Lau

9780738769820

Forthcoming Works

Visual Alchemy: A Witch's Guide to Sigils, Art & Magic
(Llewellyn, 2022)

Llewellyn's 2023 Magical Moon Calendar
(Artist, Llewellyn, 2023)

Books & Oracles

Anatomy of a Witch
(Llewellyn, 2021)

Liminal Spirits Oracle
(Llewellyn, 2020)

Weave the Liminal
(Llewellyn, 2019)

Sigil Witchery
(Llewellyn, 2018)

The Witch's Altar (with Jason Mankey)
(Llewellyn, 2018)

The New Aradia
(Editor, Revelore, 2018)

The Witch's Cauldron
(Llewellyn, 2017)

Coloring Books

Myth & Magick (2016)

The Art of Bellydance (2016)

Witch's Brew (2016)

Steampunk Menagerie (2015)

Instructional DVDs

DecoDance (2015)

Bellydance Artistry (2011)

Contributions

Llewellyn's Witches' Spell-A-Day Almanac
(Artist, Llewellyn, 2019–)

Witches & Pagans and *SageWoman* magazines
(Illustrator, BBI Media)

The Witches' Almanac, Ltd.
(Contributing author since 2017)

A Guide for the Embodied Witch

© Carrie Meyer/Insomniac Studios

About the Author

Laura Tempest Zakroff is a professional artist, author, dancer, designer, and Modern Traditional Witch based in New England. She holds a BFA from the Rhode Island School of Design and her artwork has received awards and honors worldwide. Her work embodies myth and the esoteric through her drawings and paintings, jewelry, talismans, and other designs.

Laura is the author of the best-selling books *Anatomy of a Witch*, *Weave the Liminal*, and *Sigil Witchery*, as well as *The Witch's Cauldron*, and the coauthor of *The Witch's Altar*. Laura edited *The New Aradia: A Witch's Handbook to Magical Resistance* (Revelore Press). Her first oracle deck, the *Liminal Spirits Oracle* (Llewellyn, 2020), has received much critical acclaim, including the 2021 Silver COVR award for Best Divination Product and the ITF 2021 CARTA award for Best Oracle Deck.

Laura is the creative force behind several community events and teaches workshops worldwide. Find out more at www.LauraTempestZakroff.com. Follow Laura on Instagram @owlkeyme.arts and Twitter @LTempestZ.

Anatomy of a Witch Oracle: Cards for the Body, Mind & Spirit © 2022 by Laura Tempest Zakroff. All rights reserved. No part of this book may be used or reproduced in any manner whatsoever, including internet usage, without written permission from Llewellyn Publications, except in the case of brief quotations embodied in critical articles and reviews.

First Edition
First Printing, 2022

Cover design by Shannon McKuhen
Card art, interior art, and oracle spreads by Laura Tempest Zakroff

Llewellyn Publications is a registered trademark of Llewellyn Worldwide Ltd.

ISBN: 978-0-7387-6982-0
The *Anatomy of a Witch Oracle* kit consists of a boxed set of 48 full-color cards and this perfect-bound book.

Llewellyn Worldwide Ltd. does not participate in, endorse or have any authority or responsibility concerning private business transactions between our authors and the public.

All mail addressed to the author is forwarded but the publisher cannot, unless specifically instructed by the author, give out an address or phone number.

Any internet references contained in this work are current at publication time, but the publisher cannot guarantee that a specific location will continue to be maintained. Please refer to the publisher's website for links to authors' websites and other sources.

Llewellyn Publications
A Division of Llewellyn Worldwide Ltd.
2143 Wooddale Drive
Woodbury, MN 55125-2989
www.llewellyn.com

Printed in China

A Guide for the Embodied Witch

Laura Tempest Zakroff

Disclaimer

This book contains advice and information concerning the body, mind, and spirit, and is not intended for use in order to diagnose, treat, or prescribe medical conditions or other health issues. It is not meant to replace the advice of your physician or other licensed healthcare professionals. Readers using this book and deck do so entirely at their own risk. Be mindful of any medical conditions you may have and listen to your body. The author and publisher accept no liability if any adverse effects are caused.

To Megan & Tamsin—for Secret Reasons.
Much love & gratitude.

Contents

Welcome to the Anatomy of a Witch Oracle

We have a tendency to look for influences outside of ourselves to determine our path. But more often than not, the answers we're looking for are already present within us. Or, more specifically, we are present within it, the most magnificent tool in our possession: the body. This oracle is designed to help you be more empowered in working with your body and uncovering the innate knowledge you already possess to guide you in your life. We're not just talking about your physical body here, but your magical body as well.

If you follow down a serpentine path of blood, breath, and bone—intermingled with elements and energy—the body of the Witch can be found and known. In the space between bones and muscles, nerves and blood vessels, flows the capacity for magic—a spirit being dwelling in flesh. That spirit is you. The body is a crossroads where spirit and flesh intersect. When we view the body through a magical lens, we can discover our personal power and connect more fully with the world around us.

What you hold in your hands is a unique and unusual map to help you navigate your path in a whole new way. Using both metaphysical and biological systems of the Witch's body as a guide, this oracle is a revolutionary exploration into ritual work, divination, revelation, pathworking, magic, and spellcraft.

Meet the Magical Body

To help us explore the magical body, let's begin with the metaphorical guide that I refer to as the "anatomy of a Witch." While the human body itself has numerous systems and organs—which we can definitely correlate to certain magical practices in their own way—the body of the Witch has five main parts: the lungs, heart, serpent, bones, and mind. Together they encapsulate the symbolic essence that helps direct the Witch's path.

1. With the **Witch Lungs**, we explore breath as a means to connect with others, establish embodied physical presence, maintain our sovereignty, and perceive invisible influences.

2. The **Witch Heart** provides a rhythm for us to move to as we seek balance within ourselves and with the world around us. The pulse of our blood feeds into ritual, which helps us communicate and find purpose in our work. From everyday tasks to the big moments in life, ritual plays a part in guiding our paths in so many ways.
3. Calling upon the most primal part of ourselves, the **Serpent** guides us to strengthen our powers of intuition and protection. As we trace its spiraling path, we discover the healing mysteries of creativity and transformation. We learn to trust our gut, to cleanse and protect ourselves as needed.
4. **Witch Bones** give us the strength and structure we need to build our practice. They hold the whispers of our ancestors and the spirits of the land, revealing the mysteries of death while also speaking of the future. From tradition to innovation, the Bones create the forms that help us function in the world.
5. The **Weaver** (or **Witch Mind**) is the creative cauldron that stirs everything together. It knowingly weaves together who we are from our experiences, memories, sensations, feelings, and inspirations, creating the pattern of our path.

This oracle is designed to give you deeper insight into your body—both your physical body and your metaphysical one. Whether you are looking for emotional, mental, physical, or spiritual guidance, the cards can help guide you to new perspectives on what you likely consider well-traveled territory. We are so familiar with our own body that we often take it for granted, overlooking or missing signs and signals that could give us crucial guidance. The symbolism inherent in the anatomy of a Witch can unlock those mysteries resting just below the surface, like seeds waiting to emerge. By engaging with your body more fully as a primary metaphysical tool, you will find that your magic flows so much more smoothly and effectively. The cards in this oracle invite you to consider the power of the body's different states of being, as well as magical actions, the four elements, our senses, lunar and solar influences, and traditional Witchcraft lore and magic.

About the Art

The art for this oracle pulls inspiration from my background in printmaking—the art of multiple originals crafted through serigraphy, lithography, and intaglio processes. While I mainly work in mixed media now, the history and skills that I learned while studying printmaking still heavily influence my work today.

Printmaking as an art is intricately intertwined with the evolution of human culture. From the development of symbols and written language and the refinement of crafting textiles and paper to printing presses and new matrix techniques, we can chart our capacity for creativity and innovation throughout history in these processes. Playing card games, from which the tarot developed, have printmaking to thank for their existence and ability to be more widely distributed. The same is true for alchemical engravings, mythology, and other magical lore collected into grimoires for their preservation and distribution. This booklet and the accompanying deck are another step in the ongoing relationship that printmaking has with art, spirituality, and the sharing of ideas.

The paintings in this oracle bear an uncanny resemblance to the hand-colored copperplate etchings I made in college, where I first explored themes of the body, myth, and magic in depth. Created primarily in traditional media with paper, pencil, ink, and watercolor paint, these paintings continue to explore those themes both physically and metaphysically. What separates these paintings from my college-age prints (besides process and at least two decades) is my gained experience as both an artist and a Witch. In that time, I have refined my eye, as well as my personal mythos, symbol vocabulary, and depth of practice, creating a mystical system and a vocabulary all my own.

I strived to make the imagery on the cards as accessible as possible. I want you to be able to see yourself in this art, regardless of your age, body type, gender, sexuality, etc. I hope you find it familiar as well as challenging in the best of ways.

The Body of the Deck

There are seven kinds of cards found within the 48-card deck to aid you on your journey. As with any functioning body, the cards are all interrelated, working together to bring you a more precise legend to pinpoint what needs your attention most. Some will direct you toward action, and others will ask you to stop and contemplate your current place or consider your next destination. The seven card groups are:

- Witch Anatomy
- Elements
- Senses
- Body Being

- Lunar and Solar Events
- Witch Work
- Magical Artifacts

In this booklet, for each card you will find (1) what group it's from, (2) a description of what you're seeing, (3) interpretations to consider, (4) some keywords, and (5) a prescription for the magical body. All of these aspects are designed to help you make a connection with the card, but understand that more may be revealed to you over time than just what you'll find listed here. The prescription includes suggestions to help you engage with the message of the card, but these are by no means the only ways to tap into a card.

Witch Anatomy

There are 5 Witch Anatomy cards: Witch Lungs, Witch Heart, the Serpent, Witch Bones, and the Weaver. These are the main "systems" of the magical body, together giving us the anatomy of a Witch. Each one calls attention to specific themes and practices within its domain while supporting the others.

Elements

There are 4 element cards: Air, Fire, Water, and Earth. For this deck, each element is embodied by a heart. We are made up of all four elements (united by Spirit), so these cards direct our attention to a specific element and its influence on us. The elements can also correspond to zodiac signs.

Senses

There are 6 cards for the Senses: Touch, Taste, Smell, Sound, Vision, and Perception. The senses can, of course, be interpreted very literally, but there's certainly more to discover about them. Senses can guide us in establishing protocol for our practice, deepening our perception of not only ourselves but also the world around us, and informing us on how to best apply magic in our lives.

Body Being

There are 14 cards in the Body Being group: Adorn, Align, Awake, Birth, Create, Death, Dream, Experience, Love, Maintain, Memory, Nourish, Play, and Renew. This group includes states of being as well as actions that permeate our daily lives. These cards can be very directive in helping us create change as well as understand it. They can be very mundane in their approach, but most often they're pointing to a metaphysical approach as well.

Lunar and Solar Events

There are 3 cards each for the Lunar and Solar events:

Lunar: New Moon, Waxing/Waning, Full Moon

Solar: Equinox, Solstice, Festival

These cards tap into the tides and rhythms of the cycles of the moon and our yearly journey around the sun. We can see the powerful influence of these celestial movements reflected in our lives—in our bodies, minds, and spirits.

Witch Work

There are 7 Witch Work cards that are essentially magical action or spellcraft: Banish, Bless, Cleanse, Commune, Heal, Protect, and Shapeshift. While these terms could also be applied in a mundane sense, these cards focus on magical action to bring about necessary change. They point to the kind of work we may need to do to resolve issues in our lives.

Magical Artifacts

There are 6 Magical Artifacts: Amulet, Eye, Hands, Poppet, Witch Bottle, and Witch Braid. Prevalent in spellcraft, these artifacts are often integrated into Witch work. They each have a long history steeped in magical folklore and practice. When you work with these cards, you are being asked to look more deeply at the relationship you have to that particular object or symbol, rather than taking some sort of larger magical action related to the item.

Mapping Your Journey: Using the Deck

Consider this deck very much like a map or travel guide. It can help point you to key destinations, suggest a pit stop, note important landmarks, or recommend sites to see along the way. The oracle can aid you in designing effective rituals, crafting magical workings, as well as formulating your path while refining your practice. There is no one way to use this deck. The following are suggestions to help you build a working relationship with the deck *and* your body.

Attune to the Deck

Before you begin to actively use this deck, take some time to connect with the oracle and align it with your body. Start by flipping through the cards, looking at each image briefly. Then shuffle the deck and wrap it firmly in a cloth or place it in a sturdy bag. You can use the box it came in as well, but a personalized cloth or bag not only is lighter but also adds an element of you. If you can, carry the wrapped oracle on your person (in a purse or backpack or coat pocket) when you go out into the world. For at least three nights, sleep with the deck nearby, perhaps under your pillow or bed, or you can place it on your altar if you have one. The idea is that you want the deck to have a strong connection to the rhythm of your life.

Single Card

You can pull a single card daily as a general check-in with your body—an excellent way to start your day. Before consulting this booklet, let your eyes take in the card and see what comes to mind first. If you keep a journal of your daily pulls, you can reflect upon your day and any additional information you might have received about the card. When navigating an issue, you might also pull a single card to answer a specific question, such as "What do I need to focus on?" or "What will help me move past this issue?"

Three Cauldrons Spread

The medieval Irish bardic poem "The Cauldron of Poesy" describes three spiritual cauldrons found in the human body. The Cauldron of Warming is situated just below the navel and is connected to our basic health and physical well-being. The Cauldron of Motion sits in our chest near our lungs and heart and is fueled by what inspires and drives us emotionally, creatively, and mentally. The Cauldron of Wisdom is found within or above the head and relates to our spiritual development, interconnectivity, and greater wisdom. It is said that when we are born, the Cauldron of Warming is situated upright, the Cauldron of Motion is on its side, and the Cauldron of Wisdom is inverted. Our task is to align them and keep them right side up throughout our lives.

Together, these metaphorical cauldrons can help us engage with aspects of ourselves that we tend to overlook or ignore. This three-card spread will aid you in pinpointing what you can do to address issues in the parts of the body that these cauldrons govern.

Card 1: What should I know about my body to achieve balance and improve my health?

Card 2: What do I need to do in order to stay on task or be more inspired? What emotional or mental blockages might I have?

Card 3: How do I best connect with the divine or larger vision? What will help align all three cauldrons?

Three Cauldrons spread

Along a similar theme, you could set up three cups, bowls, or cauldrons, each one devoted to a separate Cauldron of Poesy. Select a card to place in each vessel that can help you address the challenge you might be facing with that particular cauldron. For example, you might select the Fire card to go into the Cauldron of Motion to help motivate you, the Shapeshift card for your Cauldron of Warming to help you feel more comfortable in your body, and the Equinox card for the Cauldron of Wisdom to help you stay balanced, emotionally and physically.

Witch Anatomy (or Star) Spread

This spread uses the structure of the five systems of the Witch anatomy to help you devise a plan of action, assigning each area its own card, plus one more additional card that acts as the major theme or prescription. It forms a pentagram as you lay down the cards—the fivefold shape evoking the human body.

Card 1: **Witch Bones**—Foundation: where you are coming from

Card 2: **The Weaver (Witch Mind)**—What your goal is

Card 3: **The Serpent**—Messages of intuition or warning

Card 4: **Witch Lungs**—Timing, setting, or location

***Card 5:* Witch Heart**—Ritual action

***Card 6:* Center**—Overall outcome

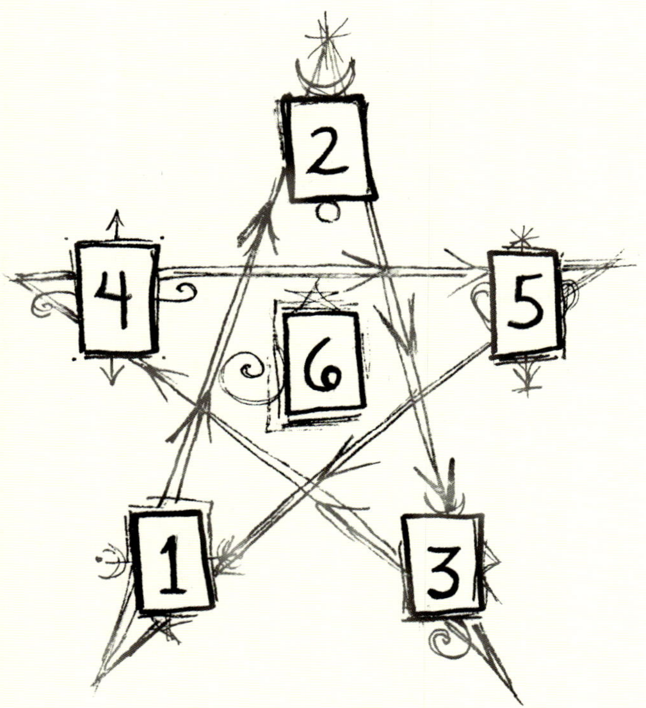

Witch Anatomy (or Star) spread

You can pull these cards from the shuffled deck for divination, or you might choose to select specific cards for every station to help create a visual representation of what you'd like to manifest. To help manifest the energy you've divined from the spread, you could gather the cards back up using an "invoking pentagram" movement. To do this, collect the cards starting with the one at the top of the star, then the one at the bottom left, middle right, middle left, bottom right, and lastly the center card.

Other Ways of Working with the Oracle

This oracle is an excellent partner deck for working with other divinatory devices. It can help you gain specific insight or clarity on what you need to do when other systems (such as the tarot, runes, bones, etc.) give you larger messages that are unclear or harder to interpret.

You can also place cards on your altar if there's a particular area or issue that you want to concentrate on. The Witch Work and Magical Artifacts groups make excellent spellcraft cards, initiating those types of motion or focus when you might not have the means or space to do something more physical (such as lighting a candle or mixing an herbal brew). You can also think of them like recipe cards, helping you coordinate a ritual or magical working.

The Journey Begins

I hope this deck helps you challenge some of the ideas you may hold about your body and brings new inspiration to your magical practice. Remember, the considerations and prescriptions for each card are starting points, not the final word on what the cards may mean or suggest. I encourage you to keep a notebook of ideas and concepts that will come to you as you continue to work with the cards in the Anatomy of a Witch Oracle, especially those that cause you to think more deeply about your senses and abilities as well as how you view your body.

Every body is different, with its own blessings, challenges, and experiences. The societies and cultures we are immersed in also influence us. Your journey as a Witch or magical practitioner is uniquely your own. Still, we have more in common together as living embodied spirits than labels and stereotypes would have us think. May this oracle help facilitate the examination of traditional ideas and their roles in our lives while opening the door to new possibilities that are ever more accessible, inclusive, and inspired.

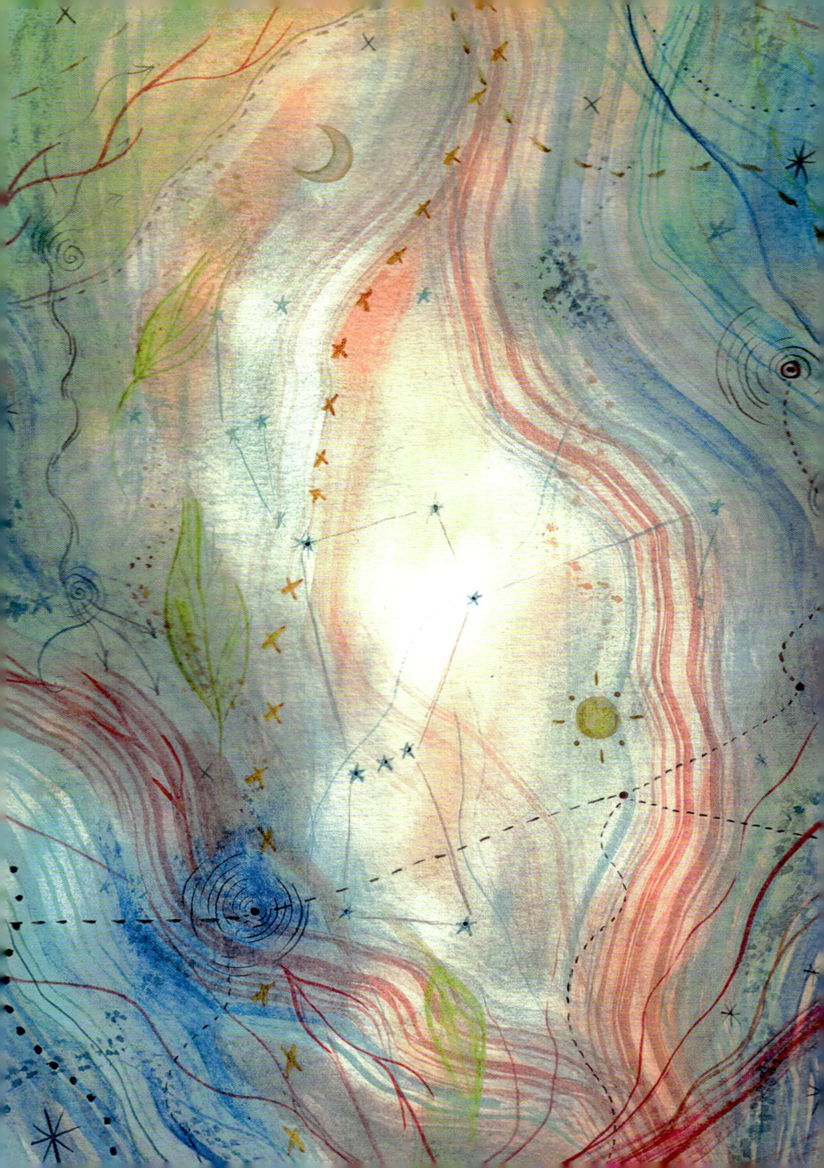

Card Descriptions

Adorn

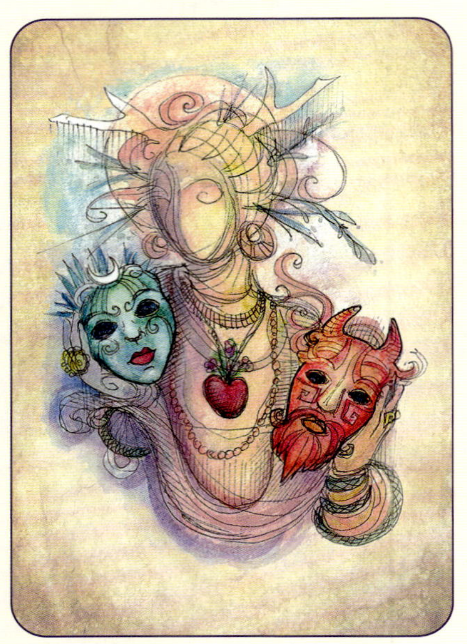

Group: Body Being

Description: An adorned golden figure holds up two masks and considers which one to choose today. Which will be their billboard to the world today? Who will they be to themselves?

Consider: There are many ways we adorn our bodies: with the clothes we wear, the jewelry we layer on, and the way we style or color our hair, as well as how we apply makeup and pierce or tattoo our skin. Each is a way to craft identity, to show the outside world how we see ourselves. We also use these items to protect ourselves, to disguise or pretend, to explore aspects of ourselves. Inversely, how we adorn our bodies can have an influence on how we feel. Adornment is a way to transform into our true self as well as a means to explore other aspects of our personality.

Keywords: Accentuate, bejewel, glamour

Rx: Look beyond a piece of jewelry or article of clothing as merely an accessory or something to wear, and consider how it transforms you. What makes you feel powerful, beautiful, present? Adorning the altar that is your body is an act of devotion. Consecrate or bless items that serve a special purpose when you wear them. Anoint your skin.

Air

Group: Elements

Description: A delicate feathered heart sails through the air, following whatever winds may guide it in this moment or the next.

Consider: The element of Air reminds us that the power of that which is invisible to us can still affect us profoundly. Air sustains life. We can feel and see the effects of air all around us even though it is invisible. Breathing is believing. Respect the unseen forces that are present in your life. Find wonder in the everyday moments of your life simply by focusing on your breath as air moves in and out of your body, connecting you to the world around you. This card can also refer to someone who is a Gemini, Libra, or Aquarius. Having a heart of Air can represent movement, lightness, transparency, impulsiveness, whimsicality, capriciousness, or being ungrounded.

Keywords: Ephemeral, effervescent, lighthearted

Rx: The direction of the wind can have metaphysical interpretations that you may use for inspiration and guidance. When the wind comes from the north, be on guard and protect. When it comes from the south, be open to receive blessings. The east wind brings new beginnings, while the west wind carries change. You might not be able to change the direction of the wind, but you can learn to sail with it.

Align

Group: Body Being

Description: Three cauldrons dance before us. Moved by Spirit, they represent the metaphorical vessels as described in the Irish bardic poem known as "The Cauldron of Poesy." At the bottom we find the Cauldron of Warming, followed by the Cauldron of Motion in the center and the Cauldron of Wisdom on top.

Consider: The Cauldron of Warming connects us to the most primal, instinctual, animal part of ourselves as well as our basic health and physical well-being. The Cauldron of Motion fuels the passion that inspires us and moves us through life. The Cauldron of Wisdom relates to our spiritual development, interconnectivity, and greater wisdom. Part of our challenge as embodied beings is tending to our internal cauldrons, balancing them, aligning them for our best well-being. Working with these metaphysical cauldrons can have very real and powerful effects on our bodies. They help us engage with aspects of ourselves that we tend to overlook or ignore.

Keywords: Coordinate, regulate, synergy

Rx: Evaluate the order and state of things around you. A little reorganization is on the agenda. If you're feeling physically out of sorts, work with your Cauldron of Warming. If you're emotionally unsettled or stressed, consult your Cauldron of Motion. If you're having trouble connecting spiritually, evaluate your Cauldron of Wisdom.

Amulet

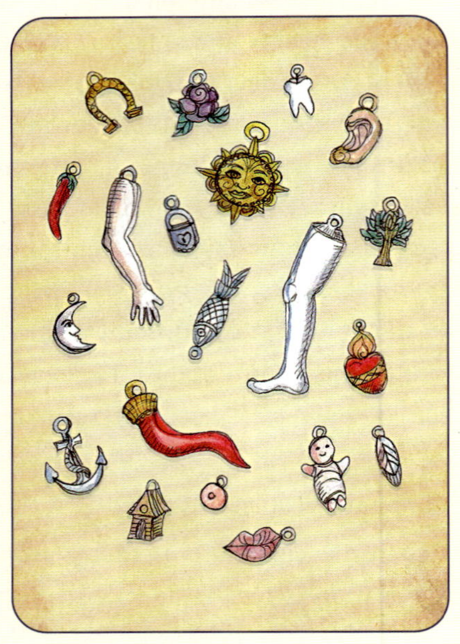

Group: Magical Artifacts

Description: Spread out before us is a wide array of jewelry charms, representing many aspects and moments of human life.

Consider: Amulets, which are commonly used to ward off negative energy, illness, and other forms of evil, have been worn by people all over the world since our earliest days. An amulet may take the form of a good luck charm, a pendant, pin, or ring, or be tucked into a bra or purse or woven into the hair. From the milagros of Spain and Mexico, the cimaruta and curved horn of Italy, and the silver veil weights of the Tuareg to the silver and gold charms found at the local jewelry store that we might give as gifts, amulets are everywhere, even if their meanings aren't universal. They symbolize relationships as well as draw good luck to us, protect us, help us commemorate and honor special moments, help us identify spiritual beliefs, and guide and heal us.

Keywords: Token, represent, enchant

Rx: Symbols have power, but what that power is depends on our relationship with the symbol and how we might utilize it. Have you noticed any symbols showing up repeatedly for you? What amulets do you cherish and why do they have power for you in your personal practice?

Awake

Group: Body Being

Description: The steam from a freshly brewed cup of tea or coffee swirls around a seated owl. The owl is perched on a large golden key and bears a keyhole in the center of its chest. A sprig of clary sage rests nearby, representing psychic insight.

Consider: It's time to be present and consider the possibilities ready to unlock themselves before you. We must draw upon our psychic powers of perception, hone our skills of observation, and physically prepare ourselves before we act. In his book *The Way of the Owl: Succeeding with Integrity in a Conflicted World*, Frank Rivers describes how the owl is an excellent role model: "In her powers of dynamic awareness, the owl is a master of the scan. By moving her attention smoothly and continuously, she builds up a comprehensive image of her situation. She gathers information broadly, deeply, and without prejudice and assembles it into a coherent whole."

Keywords: Aware, prepared, observant, engaged, clear sight

Rx: Brewed awakening: Awareness is a cumulative process. Now is a good time to pay more attention to the small, often overlooked details that make up the bigger picture. Consider how you can be more present in your daily tasks through your senses (touch, taste, smell, etc.) versus being off elsewhere in your head.

Banish

Group: Witch Work

Description: Magical action at work: a pair of scissors trims the end off of a ribbon while a piece of paper with writing on it burns in a bowl. Matches and a glass of water are standing by. In the background, a broken round mirror catches the reflection of the flames and ribbon cutting.

Consider: While some may be averse to doing banishing work, it's really part of the creation process. We are acknowledging the relationship we have to whatever we are banishing, while setting boundaries, deconstructing obstacles, or removing distractions—all of which will clear a path to new possibilities. To "uncreate" can be just as vital as creation. We can banish harmful people and situations from our lives, as well as misconceptions we have about ourselves that society has thrust upon us. Once we have cut and cleared the way, we can begin to heal, to build again, to weave a new path.

Keywords: Unbind, dissolve, dispel, eliminate

Rx: Let go of what holds you back. Reduce clutter. All of the elements can be useful in banishing and may be used in combination. Fire consumes, Earth absorbs, Water dissolves, and Air dispenses. For example, words can be written on paper (Earth) and set ablaze and reduced to ash (Fire), then released in the wind (Air) or washed away by rain or river (Water).

Birth

Group: Body Being

Description: Before us is a tunnel, with lines guiding us forward. We could be looking up into the sky from a cave below the surface. Or perhaps that's not the sky we see, but rather an egg that will soon hatch. Either way, an emergence into the world is about to happen.

Consider: There are many ways to be born, and we may experience multiple births throughout our lives—not just our emergence from the womb. Rites of initiation and dedication, coming of age ceremonies, joinings and separations are all kinds of births. Whether an emergence is physical or ideological in nature, the time spent in gestation often aids us in developing ourselves more completely. We might come out of our shell or perhaps a proverbial closet when we're ready. Maybe that shell is broken for us unexpectedly and we must go forth anyway. Regardless, keep in mind that we are working to becoming our most authentic selves throughout the whole of our lives.

Keywords: Emerge, enter, incarnate, initiate, arrive

Rx: Things are in process right now, so preparation is key. Consider how you can acknowledge the impending change or help deliver it into being. You could create ritual that focuses on building stamina and strength for endurance and/or design a rite of celebration to honor the change.

Bless

Group: Witch Work

Description: Two hands offer forth a bowl of swirling water (representing elemental Water) that is being infused with the elements of Earth, Fire, and Air. A sense of Spirit fills the air, adding intention and focus to the brew. Blessings abound as the water is shared.

Consider: To bless is to acknowledge the wonder of the world and our relationship with it. When we consecrate items for ritual and magic, we recognize their sacred importance in our lives. Even that which is usual and mundane can be appreciated and acknowledged for aiding us. A blessing is a gift freely given that carries recognition and respect. Blessings and gratitude go hand in hand. When we choose to accept blessings and practice gratitude, we shift the balance—even in dark times.

Keywords: Bestow, acknowledge, consecrate, gratitude

Rx: A daily practice of gratitude is much easier to maintain than you might think, as well as quite powerful. Choose a liminal time of day (upon waking or as you prepare to go to sleep). In your mind, acknowledge the spirits, deities, people, and/or ancestors who have helped to guide you, by name or in general. Express your thanks and choose one thing you wish to bless in your life.

Cleanse

Group: Witch Work

Description: A handmade besom is actively sweeping away debris, right out the window. All of the elements are at play here: Air, Water, Fire, and Earth. The round window gives us the illusion of a crescent moon, amplifying the cleansing energy.

Consider: Cleansing is excellent metaphysical hygiene not only for spaces and objects but for bodies as well. The cleansing process combines cleaning and spiritual intent/focus with movement, whether you're wafting smoke, anointing with water, or sweeping. Cleansing can be done to remove unwanted energies or entities, but it has other uses as well, such as preparation for a ritual. Setting aside time to cleanse your body before a ritual can align your body, mind, and spirit—setting the mood for the task ahead.

Keywords: Sanctify, purify, refresh, reclaim

Rx: Time to clean! Take a cleansing breath, bringing in fresh air and then releasing whatever is holding you down. Use a combination of the elements to clear negative energy from a room or building. Light a white candle, sprinkle some salt, utilize smoke or incense, and bless the water. Take a ritual bath or shower—cleaning the body, mind, and spirit all at once.

Commune

Group: Witch Work

Description: Three abstract spirit-like figures appear to dance around a brewing cauldron. It is hard to tell where one figure ends and the next begins, as their energies are combined—united in their purpose.

Consider: Thanks to wordsmiths such as Shakespeare, it's easy to summon the image of a coven of Witches brewing up magic around a cauldron. While a Witch may certainly work alone, working with others who share your vision can be an incredible experience. When we commune, we *come in union*—with ourselves, with spirits, with each other. In convening, we gather to conjure and create something entirely new. In the medieval Welsh poem *Preiddeu Annwn*, when we read "The first word from the cauldron, when was it spoken? By the breath of nine damsels it is gently warmed," we are reminded of the power that can be generated when we gather together and collaborate.

Keywords: Convene, collaborate, conjure, gather

Rx: Even when we're working by ourselves, we're collaborating with the world around us. Acknowledge the spirits of place and those that have come before you. When you need help, don't be afraid to ask for it. Embrace the spirit of working together to create something new.

Create

Group: Body Being

Description: Before us is a pair of hands that are both quite full. The one on the left holds a cosmic egg, with a small serpent working its way around both the egg and the hand. The egg represents the potential to create that resides in each and every one of us. The right hand holds a paintbrush, a pen, knitting needles, a seedling, and musical notes.

Consider: There are many ways to create. Whether we paint, write, play music, craft a blanket, or nurture life, we are all creators. We take of ourselves and build the world around us—with our minds, bodies, and spirits. Be careful not to fall into the trap of perfection or the idea that you need to create anything less than a masterpiece. It is the whole of our work, the collective experience of creation, that we should revel in.

Keywords: Design, originate, craft, build, conceive

Rx: Avoid waiting for the "perfect" moment to create. While there are certainly ideal conditions, creating whenever and wherever you can will yield amazing results. Harness creativity to solve problems and feel free to make multiple attempts. Make it a habit to have a small sketchbook and pen, notebook, or mobile device on hand to help you sketch and save ideas.

Death

Group: Body Being

Description: Deep within the roots of a mighty tree, we find a skeleton resting in the earth, much like we were once positioned within the womb. The main taproot of the tree grows directly out of the rib cage, while the other roots reach toward the bones, cradling the remains.

Consider: Life comes out of death, and death creates life. The tree here reminds us of Witch Lungs wisdom—that the air we breathe links us in a cycle to the plants and trees around us. Our bodies feed the trees, just as trees help to feed and house us. The tree here is rooted in the skeleton, and they embrace. In death, we understand that change is in many ways just the continuation of a cycle that started long before we took our first breath and will continue well after our last. Victor Anderson (Feri Tradition co-founder and poet) said, "Darkness lay with death and love was born." Once we cross Death's doorway, we are forever changed, yet new possibilities await us.

Keywords: Ending, changing, legacy

Rx: In our modern society, we tend to fear death rather than honor it as an important part of life. Crafting rituals for death will empower you and deepen your understanding of it. Acknowledging little deaths can help you let go of outdated ideas, old ways of life, and bad habits—and have an incredibly positive impact on your mental well-being. Celebrate the endings in your life that bring new beginnings.

Dream

Group: Body Being

Description: A figure is curled up and dreaming, their inner Serpent at rest within them as they drift in liminal space. Streaming out from them are stars of thoughts, or perhaps the stars are communicating back to them as they dream. A feline guardian is also at rest, yet it protects their person while they sleep.

Consider: Tied into the Dream card are the concepts of sleep for the body and rest for the heart, mind, and spirit. We are truly rested when we can properly experience the REM sleep cycle, which is essential for our well-being. Our deeper connection to the Serpent happens when we dream, when we can speak as well as listen to its needs and wisdom. Dreaming is a gateway to communicating with ourselves and others in other realms. Trance work can also help us achieve brain wave states similar to what we experience when we dream, so it isn't necessary to be asleep in order to travel or communicate on other planes.

Keywords: Trance, rest, travel

Rx: Although not all dreams contain a meaningful message, they do help our brains sort through our experiences and emotions. Craft a small dream pillow and fill it with herbs such as lavender, mugwort, clary sage, hops, and agrimony. Then draw a star and a snake on the fabric to finish it. Record any themes, spirits, symbols, or ideas that come to you when you awaken.

Earth

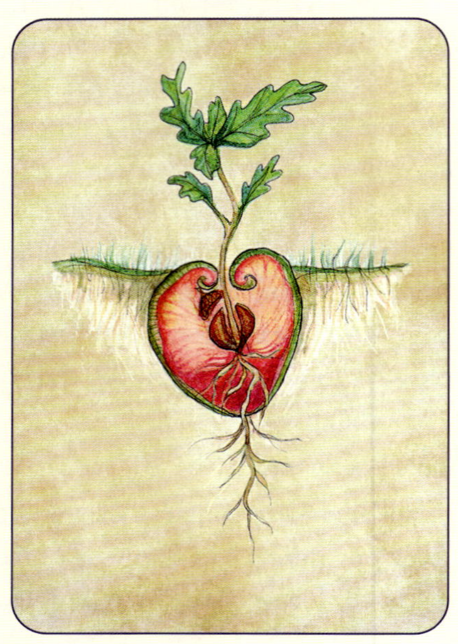

Group: Elements

Description: A heart is nestled in the earth. At the center of the heart, an acorn has begun its journey to becoming a mighty oak tree.

Consider: While our bodies contain all of the elements, we most closely resonate with Earth. But we are more than jars of clay; we are spirits in residence. In connecting with Earth, we recognize our potential for growth on multiple levels. We might start small, like the acorn, but we too can grow tall, mighty, and strong—capable of being a beacon of inspiration to others. We can lend our strength so that others may have support. This card can also refer to someone who is a Taurus, Virgo, or Capricorn. Having a heart of Earth can represent being opaque or mysterious, garden-natured (be it overgrown or tended to), supportive, resistant to change, and grounded.

Keywords: Growth-oriented, rooted, land

Rx: When you walk, kiss the earth with your feet. This means to move about the world with care, consideration, kindness, and intent. When we stomp and crash around, we risk injuring not only ourselves but others as well. Respect the spirits of place and those whose bones lie beneath your feet.

Equinox

Group: Lunar and Solar Events

Description: A sphere is split equally into bright and dark halves, balancing upon a pyramid that is also the base of a scale. On the two pans sit a Witch Heart and a feather, referencing the "weighing of the heart" ritual found in the Egyptian Book of the Dead.

Consider: Equinox means "equal night," referring to when the length of the day equals that of the night. It is a point of balance that we experience twice a year, on the first day of both spring and fall. These two equinoxes are often tied to myths about the Underworld, where the descending and ascending movements of deities like Persephone are used to explain the seasonal changes. In the ancient Egyptian ritual referenced in this card, if the deceased's heart balanced perfectly with the feather (a symbol of Ma'at, the Egyptian goddess of truth, order, and justice), the soul would be allowed to move on to the afterlife. We are in the land of the living, so we instead seek balance in our own hearts daily.

Keywords: Balance, exchange, precipice

Rx: Maintaining balance takes work and is not to be confused with preserving the status quo. Be justice-minded, practice honor, and speak with truth and respect, even if it upsets those who are comfortable with the status quo.

Experience

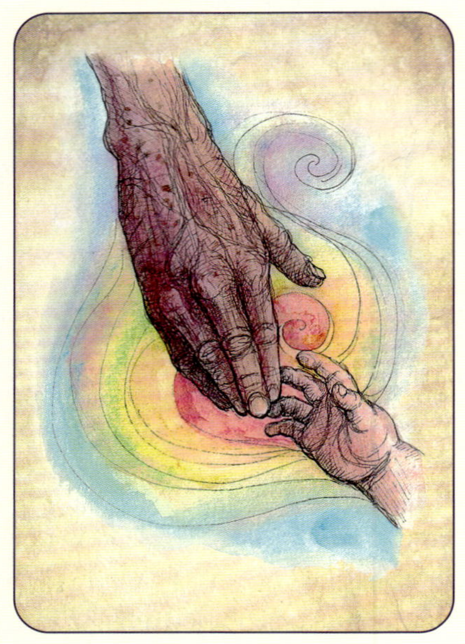

Group: Body Being

Description: A hand bearing the markings of age (swollen joints stretch over wrinkled skin dotted with spots and scars) reaches down to make contact with a child's hand. The elder will guide the young person, sharing with them what they have learned. In turn, the young invigorate, bringing new ideas and possibilities in their wake.

Consider: Experience encompasses the passing on of traditions, developing skills of survival, participating in the learning process, and the exchange of information. Witchcraft is an experiential path—you have to live the process to understand it. What you do may result in scars, but recognize those marks as symbols of moving beyond trauma, pain, and mistakes. Honor your scars, but don't be defined by them. Be bold, but also be wise. Bridge the gap between generations rather than focusing on the divide. We will all have been there at some point, if not today, then tomorrow. We are never too old to learn. If we think we know everything, we know nothing.

Keywords: Aging, earned, knowledge, undergone

Rx: Make space to listen to those who are older than you as well as those who are younger. Share your own experiences. What you do, say, and share in this world does have an impact on others, even if you're not there to observe the effects. Kindness can be a legacy all its own.

Eye

Group: Magical Artifacts

Description: A *nazar*, or evil eye amulet, is made up of layered blue glass, surrounded by a golden ribbon.

Consider: The eye of protection is found throughout the world, especially in the Mediterranean, Middle East, and Central Asia—wherever the long-held belief in the evil eye is found. *Nazar* is the most common name, deriving from the Arabic word for sight, surveillance, or attention. *Evil eye* refers to a malefic gaze (intentional or not) that causes harm to the recipient. This jealous gaze sucks the vitality out the victim and draws ill luck to them. The amulet returns the gaze to the sender, protecting the wearer—an eye for an eye. Eyes are also used to invoke the aid of deities, distract negative spirits, encourage psychic ability, and used as spiritual surveillance. This card can be a call to up your level of protection, reflect back unwanted attention, and/or pay close attention to signs around you. Another eye to consider is Odin's—he sacrificed one of his eyes to gain the knowledge of the runes. Some wisdom cannot be seen with physical sight alone.

Keywords: Behold, alert, vigilant, protection

Rx: The eye can guide us, but it can also lead us astray and fill us with envy or jealousy. Bless an eye amulet to wear or hang for protection or psychic aid. If you already have one, now is a good time to cleanse and recharge it. Anoint your brow chakra (third eye) and the center of each palm with a consecrated oil for deeper clarity.

Festival

Group: Lunar and Solar Events

Description: A path leads to a circle of standing stones, at the center of which a bonfire burns brightly as the moon begins to rise. Behind us the sun has set. The time to gather and celebrate has come.

Consider: Most festivals observe or are based on lunar or solar events, but not every special occasion is determined by the influence of the sun or moon. Birthdays, death days, and anniversaries are all events of celebration and observance as well. We hold festivals and feast days to connect to history, community, ourselves, and traditions. Festivals often revolve around ritual experiences that are ancestral, seasonal, devotional, protective, divinatory, or initiatory. Consider making a feast day of yourself, your family, or your community—you can create new traditions, find your seasonal rhythm, and take part in the continuation of history through your shared experience. It's not necessary for every event to have great meaning. Sometimes you simply feel the need to honor the experience of living.

Keywords: Celebrate, acknowledge, participate

Rx: Take notice—it's time to celebrate! Acknowledge the success in your life and honor it. What makes a festival for you? The food and drink, the music, a parade, a ritual, a dance, lights, the participants? Take three of these elements and create a spontaneous special occasion. Movement stirs joy and connects us.

Fire

Group: Elements

Description: A sacred heart of fire burns brightly before us, edged in matches that may be about to erupt into flames or perhaps have already burned. The heart is not scorched from the heat—at least not yet.

Consider: The heart is a combustible engine, driving our bodies as well as fanning the flames of inspiration. That fire can be doused with water, smothered with earth, or suffocated by a lack of air. We must be the guardians of our own fire, tending to our internal flame to keep us in motion. It is important to find a balance between prioritizing our needs and wants and supporting those around us. This card can also refer to someone who is an Aries, Leo, or Sagittarius. Having a heart of Fire can indicate someone who is passionate, all-consuming, inspiring, explosive, temperamental, or alluring.

Keywords: Passion, ignite, provocative

Rx: Working with fire requires developing an understanding that is grounded in respect. Fire can be difficult to ignite yet also very hard to control and extinguish. When you go to light a flame, center yourself, breathe, and focus on your goal. Show the same level of care when it is time to snuff out a fire.

Full Moon

Group: Lunar and Solar Events

Description: The full moon shines down upon a large body of water, the rising tide catching the light of moonbeams.

Consider: Full moons can be invigorating and inspiring, but they can also be times when we feel greater anxiety and nervous energy, sending our internal ocean into a frenzy. Rather than giving in to that chaotic energy, we can be like the ocean and reflect the light of the moon. Below the surface, we can collect and focus our energy to find a deeper sense of calm and serenity. When we summon the power within us and concentrate on our work, the moon in turn amplifies and illuminates what we do more precisely. As the *Rede of the Wiccae* says, "When the Moon rides at her peak, then your heart's desire seek." This is a prime time for magical manifestation.

Keywords: Maximum, opportunity, reflect

Rx: Whether or not the moon is actually full when you pull this card, it can signify that now is the time for magical action. It may also be a firm reminder to establish (or more consistently maintain) a monthly practice to help keep you inspired yet grounded.

Hands

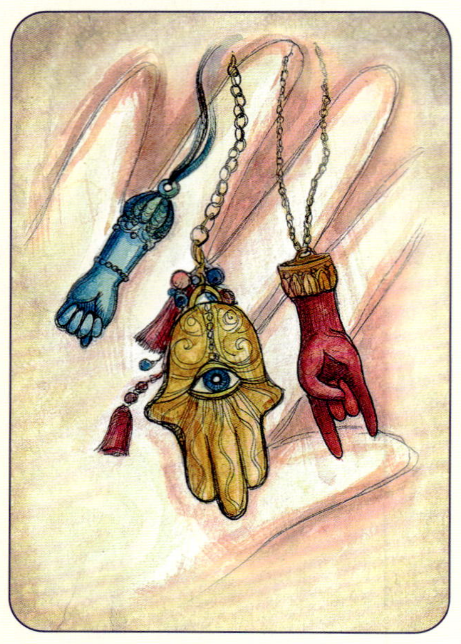

Group: Magical Artifacts

Description: In the foreground we see three hand-shaped pendants: the mano figa on the left, the hamsa in the center, and the mano cornuta on the right—all symbols of protection and power. In the background we can make out a handprint, much like those made by our ancestors thousands of years ago on cave walls and not much different from the ones we made as children with paint and paper. A handprint is evidence of existence.

Consider: Through our hands we can experience and interact with the world. We can use them to help and connect with one another, shaping community. Our hands have their own language and are steeped in symbolism all around the world. Our fingertips are critical points where the body ends and our potential to physically influence, alter, and direct the world with our intent begins. So much power rests in our hands—we can use them to build, gesture, give, receive, sculpt, speak, strum, pick, ward, write, caress, reach, protect, hold, break, and comfort.

Keywords: Impact, assistance, influence, helping hand

Rx: Forgive the pun, but it's time for a hands-on approach to whatever you've been contemplating. The best way to make your mark on the world right now is through direct interaction, getting involved, and lending aid to someone else, whether physically or metaphysically. Remember the power that rests in your hands.

Heal

Group: Witch Work

Description: A wooden staff is balanced in the earth, with a blue candle burning at the top of it. A serpent coils around the staff and kisses the flame, symbolizing the staff of Asklepios, the Greek god of healing. The Witch Heart rests just above the middle of the staff, with branches of calendula and hawthorn blossoms reaching out above it like lungs. At the base of the staff we find mushrooms and rich green leaves sprouting, while a snail glides along the surface of one.

Consider: Healing is a complicated process that requires patience. Often what makes a physical scar leaves emotional, mental, and sometimes spiritual ones as well. Even after bones are mended and bruises fade, there's more to consider below the surface. To fully heal, we must respect and honor the process and allow for growth, however long it takes. Helping others heal is an exercise in offering support and understanding what their needs are versus making our own a priority.

Keywords: Recuperate, mend, reconcile, rejuvenate

Rx: Healing comes in many forms, not just through medicinal or energetic means. Sharing food, music, and stories or even just providing a change of scenery are a few ways you could help. Honor the process, because it takes as long as it takes and that journey may take longer for some and shouldn't be rushed. Be patient and allow time for the healing.

Love

Group: Body Being

Description: Two serpents sensually intertwine with a figure that reveals a Witch Heart floating between its cupped hands. Flames start at the ground and work their way up through the center of the body, bolstering the cauldron situated at the figure's head.

Consider: Love is a force, part of magic itself. It is a sense of wholeness without demanding perfection. Love yourself, love your practice. Why? You are in a relationship with yourself. You are also in a relationship with your body, your magic, the world around you, the spirits, ancestors, deities, etc. Your practice is an entity unto itself—it has a spirit or consciousness of its own, your partner in discovering the universe. Your practice loves you. It loves the idea of you—not only you right now, but past you and future you as well. Embrace the sensual reality of being an embodied spirit, then turn your eyes to the world and fall in love.

Keywords: Passion, devotion, desire, embodied

Rx: Practice radical self-love and acceptance. Treat yourself as a lover would and embrace the beautiful possibilities. As a self-love meditation, touch or anoint your belly, chest, and forehead, saying in turn: "I open my body to love. I open my heart to love. I open my mind to love."

Maintain

Group: Body Being

Description: Down a hallway, a room is illuminated by warm candlelight and there's a hint of statuary behind a swirl of incense smoke. On the left, curtains catch the wind and sun streaming in through the window. To the right is an arrangement of cleaning supplies: a push broom, a bucket, a mop, scrubbing gloves, buckets of paint, a hammer, and some nails.

Consider: Remember, your body is a temple. In this card, we see a behind-the-scenes view of what it takes to run a temple: regular cleaning, care, and maintenance. Through a door, we see a hint of the iconic vision that often accompanies our idea of a temple. But maintaining the residence of a deity (you) also includes the less glamorous aspects that keep the temple running smoothly. If you are apt to look first for metaphysical solutions, stop and take stock of your physical wellbeing. How's your diet, sleep schedule, grooming, exercise regimen? This kind of basic maintenance, while not always glamorous as some magical work, is just as important.

Keywords: Groom, manage, conservation, upkeep, devotion

Rx: Maintaining your body is an act of devotion. Shift your perspective on the everyday tasks of eating, drinking, cleaning, grooming, dressing, undressing, etc., to see them in a more magical light. Then they become little rituals that connect you more profoundly to your body. Consider the benefits of each action and how it affects your body both physically and magically.

Memory

Group: Body Being

Description: A household shrine sits on a table. A framed photograph presides over an active candle and an incense stick, surrounded by an array of mementos. An arrangement of flowers, coins, jewelry, an antique bowl, and a raven's feather on lace suggests old stories and connections to those no longer present or perhaps someone who is just out of reach.

Consider: It's true that what is remembered lives. Memory is a multisensory experience. A whiff of fragrance, eating a certain dish, visiting an old familiar place, wearing a necklace—all of these can bring the past to life for us. Loved ones live on in our memories and dreams, embedded in our senses. But the Memory card isn't just about those who have passed on. Pictures of children, pets, and friends, mementos from trips, and cherished gifts from our partners remind us of our connections to each other and the memories we hope to create together in the future. These items and the feelings they evoke also help keep us connected, even if we're separated by many miles or time zones.

Keywords: Honor, remember, reminisce

Rx: Honoring deceased loved ones and ancestors can be as simple as wearing an item that has been passed down to you or making their favorite dish to share with others. To close the distance between you and a faraway friend or loved one, place a photo of them or a shared item on your altar. Sacred spaces can help us remember the living as well as honor the dead.

New Moon

Group: Lunar and Solar Events

Description: The new moon or dark moon is a void in the starry sky, when the moon is almost completely covered by the shadow of the earth. Below the moon, buried beneath the soil, a seed is ensconced, preparing for growth.

Consider: The moon may be barely visible in this phase, yet we know a bright crescent will soon emerge. In the absence of the moon's light, we may start to notice the brilliance of the stars in their own right. We can watch the constellations play out their stories as they travel across the night sky. Following the lead of the moon's shadowy space, we can turn our focus inward, finding the seeds of stars within us. We know not to fear the darkness, but rather to embrace it and see the curved mirror of time and space before us.

Keywords: Darkness, formulate, seed, germinate, source

Rx: Envision the darkness of the New Moon as a cloak or blanket to wear upon your soul, protecting and comforting you. Now is not the time to act, but to simply wait and observe. More will be revealed soon. This card is also a call to rest, to be gentle with yourself, and to engage in effective self-care.

Nourish

Group: Body Being

Description: A bright chalice seems to overflow like a fountain over a still life of books, fresh fruit, and other snacks. A single rose in a small vase is beginning to bloom. The flow from the cup doesn't flood or damage the books but instead symbolizes the stream of wisdom and inspiration present within the books.

Consider: "You are what you eat." There are many ways to nourish our bodies, minds, and spirits. Therefore, we need to be mindful of what we put into our bodies—be it what we eat or whatever we consume in mind or spirit. There is the nutrition we receive via food and drink and the benefit of moderation. Then there is the information we take in from the world, from others, what we consume in other ways in the form of art, music, news, and other media. Our cups can overflow with inspiration and wisdom, flowing on to others. But if we're not careful about what we absorb, we can become unbalanced or malnourished. Check the dates on what you consume—context and nuance are crucial—and some things may be past their prime.

Keywords: Cultivate, sustain, develop, influence

Rx: If you've been feeling stagnant or uninspired, it could be time to try some new flavors, activities, media, or social circles to shake things up. Challenge yourself to go outside of your comfort zone, see what's recommended by the staff at the library/bookshop, or try today's special at the café. Are you feeling lucky?

Perception

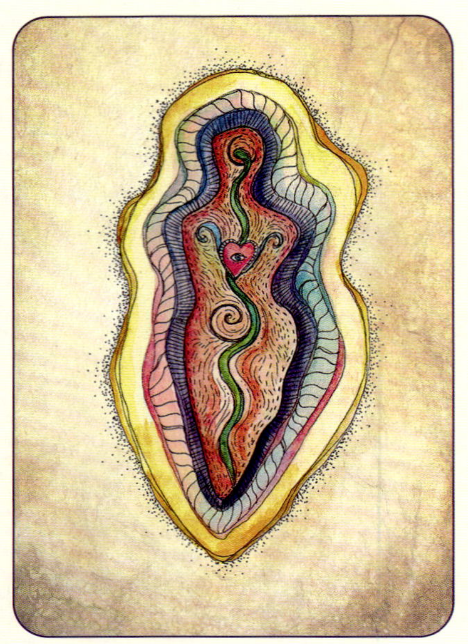

Group: Senses

Description: Almost like the view of a single cell through the lens of a microscope, an androgynous form undulates. At the center of its ethereal layers, a Witch Heart resides like a nucleus.

Consider: When people talk about a sixth sense or ESP (extrasensory perception), many consider it to be something that exists outside of our "normal" capacity for touch, taste, smell, hearing, and sight. But true perception involves all the senses layered and working together: to feel and experience with the whole of our body and being. Our bodies have evolved to be a series of diverse systems networked together for the best possible results. We can perceive simultaneously from both our outermost and innermost layers. Every single one of us has the capacity for psychic perception, and that may look different for everyone. It's also important to be careful about what we let permeate our borders and how we respond to what we perceive.

Keywords: Embodied, attunement, extrasensory

Rx: Everything is connected. This card is a reminder to perceive with the whole of yourself yet also take precautions to maintain your integrity and sovereign self. Steps you take to protect yourself physically can also safeguard you spiritually or emotionally, and vice versa.

Play

Group: Body Being

Description: What does Baba Yaga's chicken-footed hut do while the Witch is away? Play, of course! Here the Chicken Haus is off for a joyful romp with Coyote, Hare, and the Serpent.

Consider: Life can't be all about work. We need to let our imagination run free and shake out our limbs from time to time. Move, jump, dance, and flail about! Play isn't just for the body, either. It's for the mind as well. Allow for some fantasy, suspend disbelief on occasion, and let yourself fly. Go ahead and engage in a little make-believe. When we allow ourselves to play, our mind relaxes and our view shifts, allowing for greater problem-solving capabilities. Worry less about what others think and resolve to play more. Dance like no one is watching. Be ridiculous and full of wonder. Make some myths and memories now.

Keywords: Imagination, spirited, mischief, revel

Rx: Play can take the form of relaxing at the beach, hiking in the woods, and role-playing with friends, or it might mean making a game out of tasks you've been avoiding. Shifting your perspective changes the scenery and opens doors you didn't even know existed.

Poppet

Group: Magical Artifacts

Description: Three different kinds of poppets are on display: a corn dolly, a figure fashioned from roots and branches, and a vibrantly colorful embroidered fabric form.

Consider: Poppets have long been used in sympathetic magic practices to represent people or other living beings. They are generally for casting spells on the subject they are modeled after—to aid them or to work against them. These effigies can also act as ritual stand-ins and function as spirit residences. Poppets can be made from a wide variety of materials, including fabric, paper, branches, roots, leaves, flowers, clay, wax, and pretty much any other substrate that can be easily fashioned into a form. From there they may be stuffed with herbs, hair or nail clippings from the target, clothing acquired from the person, or anything else that helps connect the poppet to its living or spiritual correspondent. Poppets can be used to deflect negative energy or issues, as well as act as guardians or guides.

Keywords: Votive, encapsulate, channel, transfer

Rx: Not everything has to be done directly through you or your body. While you may want to control everything, not everything has to be on you. It's time to delegate some authority, share the workload, accept assistance from others, and take care to keep some energy in reserve.

Protect

Group: Witch Work

Description: A deer skull is encircled by rue, mugwort, rosemary, and star anise. A five-pointed star is displayed between the antler prongs, made up of a red ribbon that weaves down and through all of the herbs.

Consider: One of the most fundamental and essential forms of magic is protection work. Protection has many forms and functions: defending, preventing, preparing, ensuring safety, creating secrecy, securing space, etc. Some protective things we must make a conscious choice to use (like an oven mat), while others (such as a nazar amulet) do the work without us even having to think about it. Protection means checking our defenses, establishing wards, connecting with guardians, maintaining good spiritual health, and making sure we're prepared for the repercussions of our own actions. We must also consider what it is we are looking to protect. Sometimes we put our guard up when we need to be more open simply because we're afraid or uncertain. Use your skills of perception to tell the difference between friend and foe.

Keywords: Defend, keep, encircle

Rx: Daily protection is vital to magical living yet far too easy to forget about. You can anoint yourself with an oil of protection or blessed water, wear a consecrated amulet, or maintain a practice of mobile sacred space. There is nothing wrong with maintaining your boundaries.

Renew

Group: Body Being

Description: A large empty, broken eggshell rests in a nest of frayed rope and shed snakeskin. The rosy hue in the sky suggests that it may be dusk or dawn. From the sky fall feathers and what appear to be petals or perhaps particles of ash. Whoever was in the egg or wore the skin has already moved on.

Consider: The Serpent guides us through the wonders of transformation, renewal, and regeneration. So many myths speak of the Serpent's abilities to create the world, to take of itself and refashion everything. Similarly, the Phoenix, whose feathers and ash fall from the sky, reminds us that rebirth is always possible. It's time to shed that old skin, to break the ties that have held you back, whether they were imposed by yourself or others. Emerge as your most authentic self ever. Set the world ablaze with the new you. You just need to release the ideas and fears that have weighed you down.

Keywords: Regenerate, replenish, release

Rx: Wriggling out of an old skin isn't easy—it can be hard to see where you're going and feel messy. This card is a sign that even though things may seem difficult, trust your intuition and keep moving forward. A bathing ritual to banish and cleanse can help remove lingering debris or obstacles, clearing the path ahead.

The Serpent

Group: Witch Anatomy

Description: A powerful verdant serpent undulates before us, forked tongue tasting the air as it surveys future paths.

Consider: Cradled within your pelvis, a serpentine energy is coiled, biding its time. The most primal part of ourselves, the Serpent, guides us to strengthen our powers of intuition and protection. As we trace its spiraling coils, we discover the healing mysteries of creativity and transformation. Through the wisdom of the Serpent we learn how to shed our skins, soak up the sun when we need to rest, and strike when in danger. There is nothing to fear here—this is an integral part of your path, the wild part of you that has always been there and has never forgotten magic. The path ahead will have its curves and shifts, and you'll move right along with it.

Keywords: Primal self, intuition, creatrix

Rx: Learn to trust your gut. Practice both stillness and movement. For stillness: focus on your breath, relax, quiet your mind and body. Take in the world around you without reacting—just watch. Then begin to move slowly and be sensuous and present. Focus on how it feels to gently move and stretch different parts of your body. Breathe.

Shapeshift

Group: Witch Work

Description: Intersecting colorful spheres display a menagerie of beasts. An amber-eyed black cat stares directly out at us. Around her we see an owl, the coils of a snake, the tail of a fish, a spider, a toad, a hare, and a goat. It's hard to tell where one ends and the next begins as their shapes intermingle.

Consider: Folklore is full of Witches and other magical practitioners who are said to be able to shapeshift into animals—especially for flying to sabbats or making mischief. Whether these transformations are actually physical or more of a spiritual nature, there is no denying our animal selves. Recognizing that we are interconnected with the world brings us closer to nature and to the wild, mysterious, and uncharted parts of ourselves. Our spirits can contain a diverse array of traits and features that may come out depending on where we are and who we are with. We may walk in multiple worlds—and not all of them are of a magical nature. Shapeshifting speaks to our ability to contain multitudes, to code-switch, to not be reduced to labels and stereotypes. Speech, movement, and dress all factor into shapeshifting. Playing with disguise can not only protect us but also help us see the world in new ways.

Keywords: Transformation, versatility, metamorphosis, chimera

Rx: Ask yourself, "Who am I really? How does the world see me versus how I see myself?" You truly contain multitudes, and there is no shame in being hard to pin down. For as many eyes that see you, there are even more versions of you perceived by others. Find the shape that makes *you* feel at home, even if it's something you explore only on special occasions or with certain people.

Smell

Group: Senses

Description: Two beautiful glass Egyptian perfume bottles stand surrounded by jasmine blossoms, while a nearby brass incense holder releases swirling waves of smoke.

Consider: Our sense of smell is deeply linked to memory. This connection likely evolved from our early survival instincts—our need to be able to detect danger from predatory animals, bad food, or shifting weather, as well as remember what foods are good and what places are safe. Scent also plays a huge role in attraction—who we are drawn to or repulsed by—all through the power of our noses! With the combined powers of Earth, Fire, and Air, we use smoke to cleanse as well as perfume spaces, and also to communicate with spirits, deities, and ancestors.

Keywords: Fragrant, aroma, pungent

Rx: Scent can have an impact on your state of mind (hopefully beyond any allergies). Applying a familiar scent to your body can bring comfort, burning certain kinds of incense can lift your spirits, and getting some fresh air, regardless of the temperature outside, can awaken your mind. Make note of which smells empower and inspire you so that you can tap into those energies for ritual.

Solstice

Group: Lunar and Solar Events

Description: A pair of light and dark spheres work opposite each other. Between the spheres, we see a city and a forest from the perspective of a *camera obscura*—where the outside world is reflected through a pinhole of light into a dark room and appears completely inverted. Here, instead of seeing the usual reverse image, we have a city and a forest in balance.

Consider: The solstices mark both extremes of the year yet also are points of balance. The Winter Solstice has the longest night and the shortest day, while the Summer Solstice has the reverse. Solstices remind us that light and dark define each other, always in a dance of balance. As soon as we reach the farthest point, we dance back to the center and beyond again. We are forever seeking a balance between the wild and domesticated parts of ourselves.

Keywords: Consummation, capacity, juxtaposition

Rx: Know that balance isn't always about equal halves, but about momentum and perception as well. Highs and lows have their power, too. Sometimes being "extra" is exactly what is needed to get things on track. In ritual, play with the concepts of "less is more" and "more is more."

Sound

Group: Senses

Description: A brass bell hangs, adorned with a bat design. The tassel attached to the clapper is in motion—perhaps the bell was just rung or the wind itself will ring it soon. Nearby are ginkgo biloba leaves and blossoms of St. John's wort, herbs used to aid with hearing.

Consider: Percussionist Evelyn Glennie once said, "Hearing is a form of touch," which acknowledges the fact that often we feel sound as much as we hear it—and some of us even see sound! For example, consider that the bat gracing our ringing bell uses echolocation to "see," or imagine the pulse of a bass amp at a concert. In ritual we may ring bells, beat drums, or use our voices to clear and awaken a space, call upon deities and spirits, and enter trance. An inherent part of sound is the art of listening, of becoming in tune with our surroundings and those around us. Glennie also said, "Silence is the loudest sound." Sometimes it's what we *don't* hear that matters more and should draw our attention.

Keywords: Resonance, harmony, reverberation

Rx: We hear things differently in our own skulls, which is wise to keep in mind when communicating with others. Sometimes we accidentally create dissonance because we all don't hear in the same way or maybe we missed part of the message. To reach harmony with others, seek clarity and then listen carefully to what's being said (or left unsaid).

Taste

Group: Senses

Description: A serpent's tongue is shadowed by a honeycomb shaped like a human tongue and surrounded by a honeybee, hot peppers, a bowl of salt, a sprig of mint, and lemons still on the tree branch.

Consider: Taste is discernment. A snake uses its tongue to taste the air, decide where to go next, and explore the world. Honey, peppers, salt, mint, lemon—all of these flavors activate different taste buds on the tongue. The honey tastes rich and sweet, the pepper hot and spicy, the mint cool and tingly. The lemon puckers with sour acid and the salt makes our mouth water. When you speak, are your words spicy, salty, or perhaps sweet like honey? Does what you say add richness to a conversation, or are you seeking to sour the tone? The tongue is a powerful muscle, and words do indeed have power. Be careful with what you say and how you say it. The words you speak, you also consume.

Keywords: Savor, discernment, sensitivity, discretion

Rx: Be a tastemaker. If you have something to say, and the way your idea is received by others is vital to your success, then harness the power of sympathetic magic by eating something that correlates to the desired response. You can also turn to kitchen witchery to cook up a delicious dish to share with your intended audience to help sweeten (or spice up) the reception.

Touch

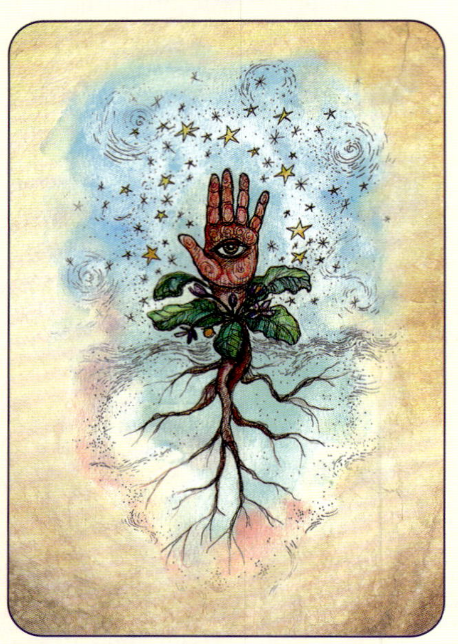

Group: Senses

Description: A hand with an eye situated in the center of its palm emerges up out of a thriving mandrake plant. The hand touches the sky and stars while still being firmly rooted and deeply connected to the earth.

Consider: Throughout our bodies is woven an extensive system of nerves. Many of those nerve endings are situated in our hands as well as our feet, collecting a great deal of information for the brain. Through just a touch we are able to recognize temperature, hard versus soft, slick versus rough, receptive versus resistant, and much more. Our sense of touch has a major impact on how we physically navigate through the world. If we push too hard and too fast, we can quickly become off-balance. When we move from our core, our actions are more rooted and stable. Another aspect of touch is understanding consent and sovereignty. Preferences on how, where, when, why, and by whom someone is touched depend on the individual and are not universal. Always ask permission and never assume.

Keywords: Contact, advocate, interact

Rx: Respecting the power of touch applies to more than just humans. Consider the best possible ways to make contact with plants, animals, and spirits as well. Be mindful of the strength of your touch and aware of how it might affect others.

Vision

Group: Senses

Description: An alert eye gazes back at us, shedding a single tear. Before it rest belladonna blossoms and berries as well as a skeleton key with a ribbon. A shaft of blue-violet light connects the eye to the berries, forming a keyhole shape with the pupil. The swirls around the eye are also reminiscent of the Eye of Horus.

Consider: Vision is one of the senses we depend on the most, yet it can be one of the least dependable. The brain is constantly filtering the information from the visual cortex, determining what we see. Insights from our other senses combined with psychic perception can help us see the bigger picture. Sometimes we need to soften our gaze to uncover secrets. Also remember that seeing always isn't believing and glamour may be afoot to distract your gaze. Beauty is very much in the eye of the beholder—which reminds us that with vision, we need to consider what we see as well as how we are being seen.

Keywords: Insight, revelation, visible

Rx: Vision is more than physical sight. It's also being able to reflect on the past through the lens of experience to gain a better understanding. It's the gift of being able to imagine the future framed by the illumination of hope and possibility. Consider scrying to activate a different part of your inner sight to divine hidden meaning.

Water

Group: Elements

Description: A heart peeks out from a moon snail shell, with bubbles and wisps surrounding it, resembling a chambered nautilus navigating its way through the water with its many tentacles.

Consider: Water cleanses, purifies, dissolves, and submerges. Our bodies contain an ocean of us, ever in motion and influenced by the lunar tides. With water, boundaries can blur easily and quickly and sometimes we can get swept away in the moment. When exploring new magical practices or emotional territory, have a fixed goal in mind to keep you steady. It is up to you to swim, float, or sink. This card can also refer to someone who is a Pisces, Cancer, or Scorpio. Having a heart of Water can indicate someone who is full of emotion, nurturing, secretive, fluid, flowing, absorbing, graceful, swift, receptive, or unpredictable.

Keywords: Aquatic, seaworthy, fluidity

Rx: Drinking water is the perfect way to finish a ritual or magical working. Hold a cup of fresh water in your hands, close your eyes, and take three breaths, focusing on the Serpent, the Witch Heart, and the Weaver in turn. Then drink the water, conscious of the taste, and feel as it enters your body. Water can also be an easy yet effective offering.

Waxing/Waning

Group: Lunar and Solar Events

Description: Here we see two crescent moons gathering and releasing energy. Which moon is waxing and which one is waning depends on the hemisphere you live in.

Consider: From the new moon to the full moon, we can gaze upon the waxing crescent. From the full moon to the new moon, we see the waning crescent. When we work with the ebb and flow of the lunar tides, we can amplify the work we do. Tap into the lunar rhythm of ebb and flow, collect and disperse, increase and decrease. With the power of the lunar tides, what will you build and create and what will you release and let go of?

Keywords: Becoming, turning, vanishing

Rx: Learn how to flow with the lunar tides. Work with the waxing moon when you need to build or increase and with the waning moon when you're looking to decrease or diminish. But if something needs to be done right away and the moon doesn't seem to be moving in your favor, consider how to shift your focus. For example, when the moon is waning, instead of designing a healing spell to draw good health, you could work to decrease the barriers or factors that are impeding good health.

The Weaver

Group: Witch Anatomy

Description: A sturdy cauldron releases a mighty vision of fiery flames that weave together to form a five-pointed star. From each point of the star, tendrils float outward, reminiscent of nerve cells.

Consider: The Weaver (or Witch Mind) is in charge of consolidating, synthesizing, and communicating the information derived from the rest of the Witch anatomy—collecting, organizing, and disseminating threads. It is a cauldron of creativity, a problem solver, a designer, mission control, and a conduit for Spirit. The Witch Mind is the guiding star that illuminates the path before us. Within the threads of the Weaver we find the primary network of communication between ourselves and the universe. The Weaver reminds you that *you* are the spirit in control of your body. You have all the information you need—now it's time to make your choices and weave a pattern worthy of you. Just be careful not to spend too much time up in your head!

Keywords: Self-divine, transmission, command central, gateway

Rx: Remember to check in with the whole of your body. Take a breath and feel the beating of your heart, the warmth of your belly, the solidness of your bones, the star upon your brow. This is your story to tell. Guide the way with integrity.

Witch Bones

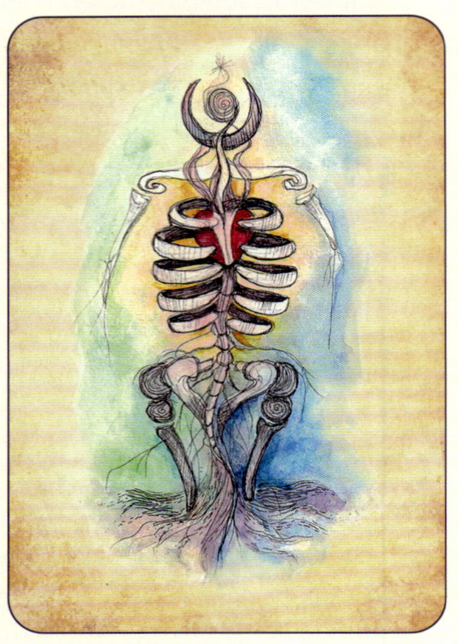

Group: Witch Anatomy

Description: A skeleton, protecting a heart, seems to be interconnected by threads that reach up to a crescent moon resting where the skull would normally be as well as down into the surface from which the bones are emerging.

Consider: Witch Bones give us form, structure, and strength to build our practice on as we craft tradition. They remind us of the liminal space between life and death, bringing us the wisdom of the ancestors. Witch Bones tell us the stories that become the songs we sing in this life and carry on to the next. The Earth below our feet is made up of those who have come before us and sets the space that we share with others. Our bones give us shape, protect our internal organs, and aid us in mobility. We are the ancestors of tomorrow, with our roots touching the past and our hearts embracing the present. Tradition is being crafted every moment. Our relationship with the land is a never-ending story.

Keywords: Structure, foundation, roots

Rx: No matter where your family or practice is from, reach out and connect with the spirits of place and the land beneath you. They will support you. Also, not all long-held traditions grow with us—some hold us back or can even cause damage. Don't be afraid to innovate and move forward.

Witch Bottle

Group: Magical Artifacts

Description: A large corked and wax-sealed bottle is full of a mysterious liquid and other items, while a smaller bitters bottle stands nearby. An array of Witch balls hang above them.

Consider: Depending on the folklore, Witch balls and bottles are made by Witches and magical practitioners but also can be procured and used to ward against curses thrown by them. A Witch bottle might contain urine, vinegar, hair, fingernail clippings, red thread, thorns, coins, ash, nails, pins, salt, blood, red wine, or herbs. Witch bottles are typically buried on the edge of a property or hidden somewhere within a home to capture and contain evil forces. Witch balls are decorative glass spheres that are prominently hung in windows to ward off bad luck and evil spirits. They are not usually filled with anything like what is found in a Witch bottle, but instead the colors, patterns, and shapes made by the glass do the apotropaic work.

Keywords: Fascinate, distract, mesmerize

Rx: In many ways, both Witch bottles and balls are meant to redirect attention. Are you being distracted by others, leading to disruptions in your work? If so, you could construct a Witch bottle or hang a Witch ball in your work area to deflect any unwanted energies.

Witch Braid

Group: Magical Artifacts

Description: A length of hair and some strands of fiber have been braided into a rope that features three embellished stations of knots, adorned with feathers, beads, twigs, buttons, and bells.

Consider: Braids bring together disparate elements to create something new and unified. A Witch ladder is a traditional folk magic practice where a spell is constructed from knotted cord or braided hair. Charms, feathers, and other items are knotted or braided in with specific magical intention to create a cord. The number of knots, braided elements, and charms varies depending on the tradition and purpose, with three, nine, and thirteen knots being the most common. In some traditions, every knot stores power, holding the spell until it might need to be undone. Our desire to braid and knot can also reflect our need to control a situation. Sometimes we just need to let our hair down, be free and loose, and let go of the need to control.

Keywords: Intertwine, weave, hold fast

Rx: To help gain control over a situation, work a braid into your own hair. If hair isn't an option, braid or knot embroidery floss into a bracelet or anklet to wear. Consider the color, materials, and size carefully and maintain your focus as you work. Be specific and intentional about your choices.

Witch Heart

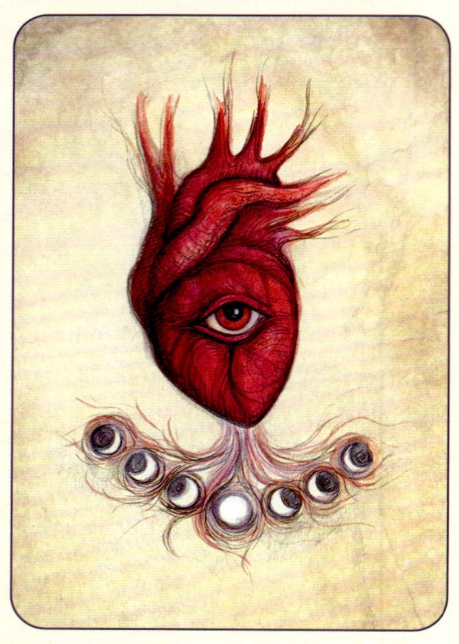

Group: Witch Anatomy

Description: A large eye gazes calmly at us from the center of an anatomical human heart. At the base of the heart, blood vessels surround seven spheres that represent the lunar cycle.

Consider: The Witch Heart sets the pulse for our practice, awakening our emotions and granting us vision to direct the path ahead of us. It asks us to think about not only what stirs us into motion but also what keeps us moving. Ritual is the realm of the Witch Heart, helping us find the rhythm in the big moments as well as everything in between. Think about how time and pattern are essential for establishing rhythm: day or night, simple or complex, lunar or solar, regular or spontaneous. We tend to think of ritual as being for the big, dramatic moments in life, but daily practice is built on the strength of small moments.

Keywords: Ritual, pattern, rhythm

Rx: What moves you? Have you made room lately for your own passions, or are you getting swept away in the rush of everyday life and other people's needs? Take a close look at your heart and consider what your needs are and how you can start achieving your goals. An effective daily practice is made up of the things we find power and personal meaning in—and that might not look like anyone else's path. Honor your heart.

Witch Lungs

Group: Witch Anatomy

Description: Clusters of flowers, greenery, and fungi form a pair of lung shapes, which feed up into a mighty tree. All of the seasons are present in the tree's branches.

Consider: With every breath, you bring the outside world inside of you. With every exhalation, you share molecules of yourself with the world. The Witch Lungs teach us that everything and everyone is interconnected. However, this connection doesn't mean you yield your personal sovereignty. You are in control of your own domain, your body, and what you put out into the world. Own your breath, recognizing your own sovereignty and power. There is a balance between what you take from the world and what you put into it. There is a season for everything, if you take the time to observe and seek to understand the patterns of life happening around you.

Keywords: Interconnection, sovereignty, creating space

Rx: The Witch Lungs share the wisdom of understanding what in our lives is permeable and shared with the world and what should be protected and kept for just us. Be mindful of what you take from and give to others. Use your breath as a metaphysical filter by focusing on what you wish to both breathe in and release out into the world.

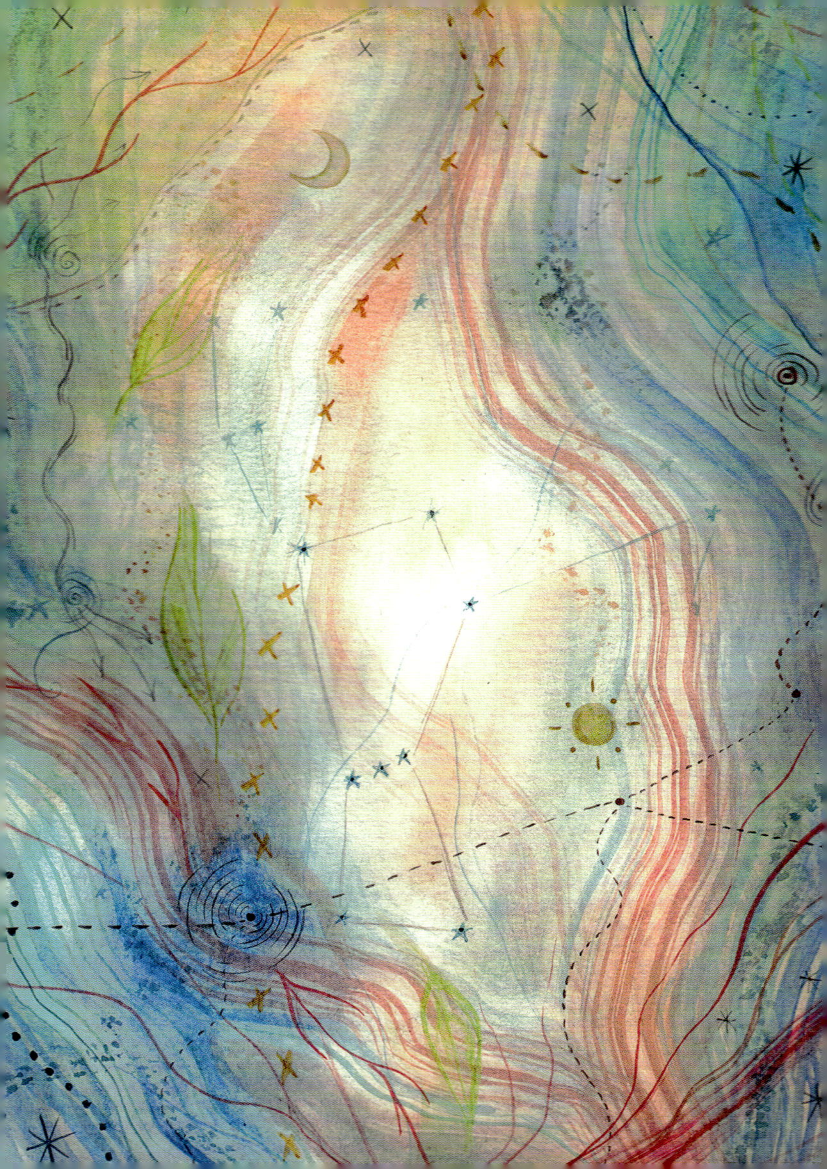

Sources Cited

(Awake) Rivers, Frank. *The Way of the Owl: Succeeding with Integrity in a Conflicted World* (San Francisco, CA: Harper Collins, 1997), 112.

(Commune) Graves, Robert. *The White Goddess: A Historical Grammar of Poetic Myth* (New York: Farrar, Straus and Giroux, 1986), 107.

(Death) Anderson, Cora. Victor Anderson quoted in *In Mari's Bower: A Biography of Victor H. Anderson* (Portland, OR: Harpy Books, 2012), 63.

(Full Moon) Mathiesen, Robert, and Theitic. *The Rede of the Wiccae: Adriana Porter, Gwen Thompson, and the Birth of a Tradition of Witchcraft* (Providence, RI: Olympian Press, 2005), 52.

(Sound) *Touch the Sound: A Sound Journey with Evelyn Glennie*, directed by Thomas Riedelsheimer (Germany: Piffl Medien GmbH, 2004).

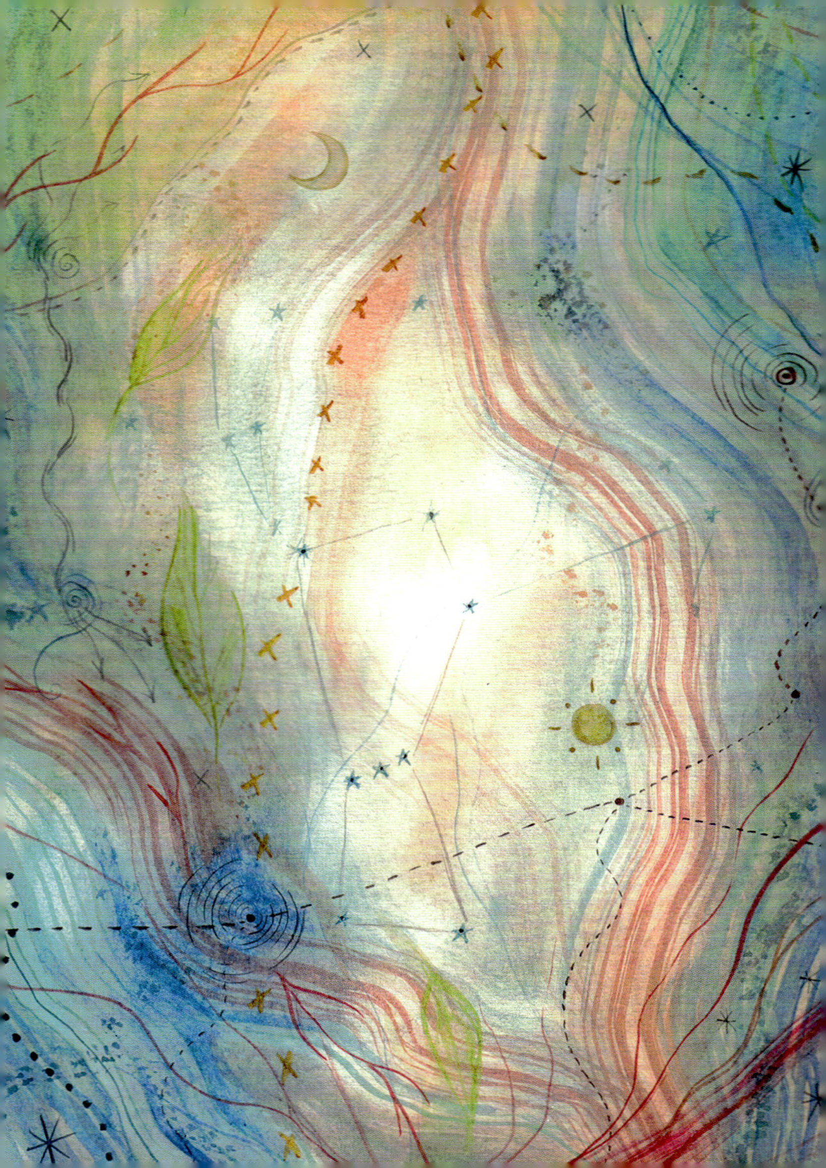

Recommended Reading

The following books by Laura Tempest Zakroff will help you dive deeper into many of the unique concepts related to this deck.

Weave the Liminal guides you through what it means to be a modern Witch. It helps you to craft a personalized practice of Witchcraft that incorporates your roots, daily living, inspiration, environment, and much more. Through these insights, you'll be able to weave together the threads of your life in order to make a strong pattern that reflects your experience and goals. Llewellyn, 2019.

Anatomy of a Witch is the book that this oracle is based on. It builds upon the concepts found in *Weave the Liminal* and guides you to truly embody your practice. Each part of the magical body is explored in great detail, along with exercises, rituals, and sigils to help you connect with each. Llewellyn, 2021.

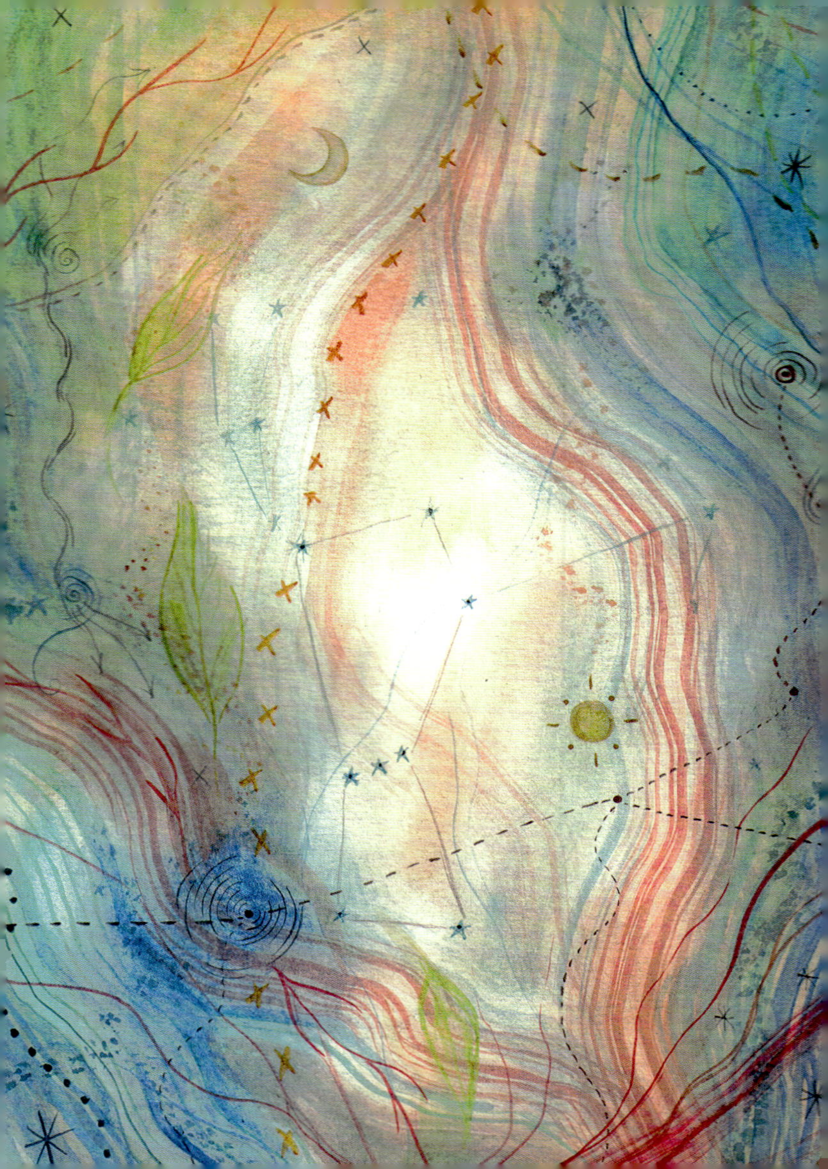

To Write to the Author

If you wish to contact the author or would like more information about this book, please write to the author in care of Llewellyn Worldwide Ltd. and we will forward your request. Both the author and the publisher appreciate hearing from you and learning of your enjoyment of this book and how it has helped you. Llewellyn Worldwide Ltd. cannot guarantee that every letter written to the author can be answered, but all will be forwarded. Please write to:

Laura Tempest Zakroff
℅ Llewellyn Worldwide
2143 Wooddale Drive
Woodbury, MN 55125-2989

Please enclose a self-addressed stamped envelope for reply, or $1.00 to cover costs. If outside the U.S.A., enclose an international postal reply coupon.

Many of Llewellyn's authors have websites with additional information and resources. For more information, please visit our website at http://www.llewellyn.com.

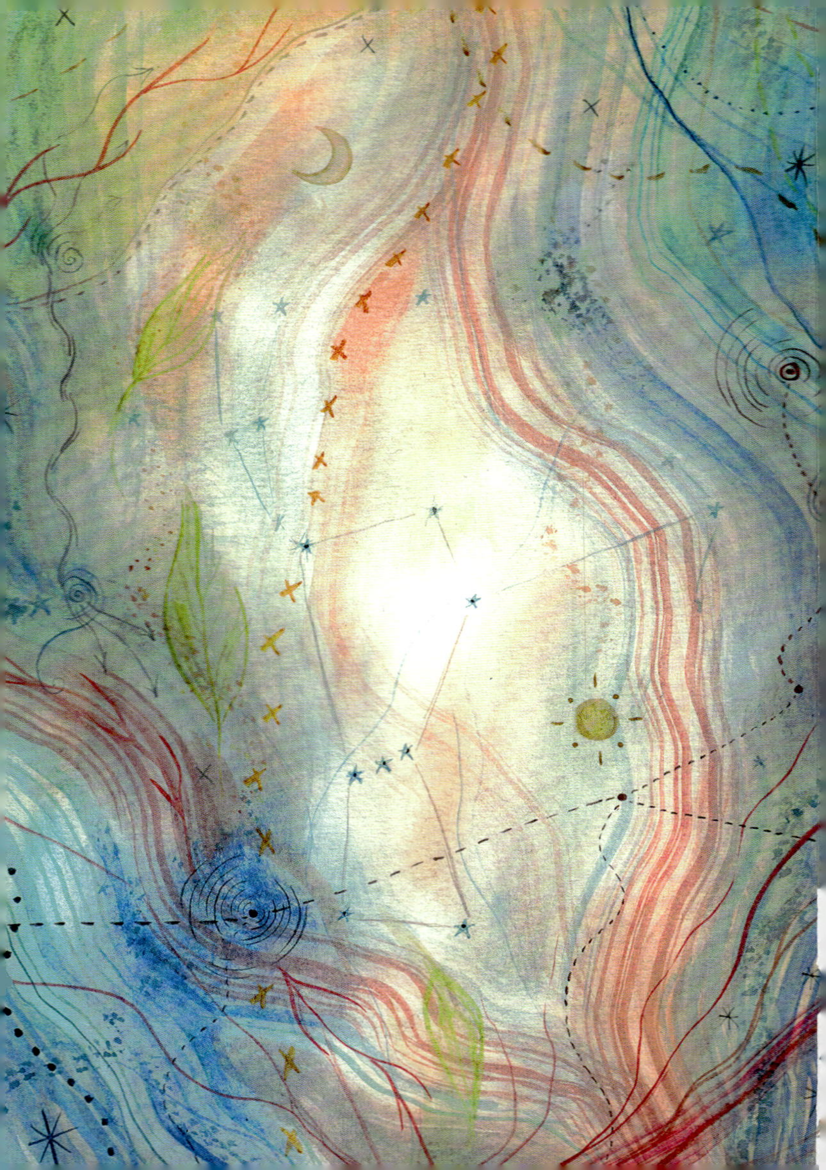